An Eye on Hong Kong

Tai O, Lantau

1995

Dragon boat races shot at a slow speed to convey the movement and excitement of this boisterous, colourful event.

PREVIOUS PAGE
The Harbour

1998

Hong Kong's best-known panorama, from Lugard Road on the Peak, encompasses (in the foreground from left to right) Central, Wanchai and Causeway Bay on Hong Kong Island, and (in the distance) Kowloon on the north side of Victoria Harbour, Hong Kong's greatest asset has always been its magnificent natural sheltered harbour, now home to one of the world's busiest container ports and visited by over 175,000 ocean-going vessels a year. For over a hundred years, land reclamation has been slowly encroaching on the harbour, bringing the waterfronts of Tsim Sha Tsui and the island's north shore closer together. Today, almost every building on the island's north shore is on reclaimed land, and the ever-quickening pace of reclamation is giving some environmentalists and almost all the population of Hong Kong cause for extreme concern.

OVERLEAF
Causeway Bay Typhoon Shelter

1998

A stunning August sunset provides the backdrop to Central, North Wanchai and the Causeway Bay Typhoon Shelter. The Island Eastern Corridor snakes along the shoreline, and the office blocks of North Wanchai sparkle with extraordinary reflections. The craft moored in the shelter are a mix of two extremes: the expensive yachts owned by members of the Royal Hong Kong Yacht Club contrasting with the small sampans and working fishing boats which base themselves in the typhoon shelter. The new Hong Kong Convention and Exhibition Centre is in the right centre.

Sha Tin Races, Ladies' Day

1996

The public stands are packed to capacity. Without doubt horse racing is Hong Kong's most popular sport, mainly because it is the only legal form of gambling here. The Hong Kong Jockey Club was founded in 1884 but professional racing was not introduced until 1971. In the 1995/6 season the betting turnover was a staggering HK$80.7 billion of which 81% was paid back to punters in dividends, 12.8% in duty and HK$1.1 billion was donated to charity and sports organizations.

PREVIOUS PAGE

The Island

1998

Taken from the new reclamation next to the Western Harbour Crossing this spectacular view of Hong Kong's north shore stretches from the new Cosco building and "The Center" on the right to North Wanchai and the Hong Kong Convention and Exhibition Centre on the left.

INSIDE GATEFOLD

Festivals

A colourful collection of photographs taken at various festivals around Hong Kong.

OVERLEAF

Lamma Island

1990

Sunset over Lamma Island from Headland Road. This view has remained unchanged for 25 years with just two notable exceptions: on the right is Ocean Park's rollercoaster, just one of the excitements offered by the 160-acre marine park which opened in 1977; and on Lamma Island an electric power station, with its prominent smoke stacks, which was built in 1980.

AN EYE ON HONG KONG

A PORTFOLIO OF PHOTOGRAPHS

1 9 7 0 – 1 9 9 8

BY KEITH MACGREGOR

FOREWORD BY SIR DAVID AKERS-JONES

PUBLISHED BY PACIFIC CENTURY PUBLISHERS LTD.

ISBN 962-217-597-X

First published in Hong Kong in 1997 by Cameraman Ltd.
This edition published in 1998 by Pacific Century Publishers Ltd.

All enquiries to:
Pacific Century Publishers Ltd.
1003 Kowloon Centre, 29-43 Ashley Road, Tsimshatsui, Kowloon, Hong Kong
Tel: 2376 2085 Fax: 2376 2137 E. mail: airman@gateway.net.hk

Photography by Keith Macgregor ©
Picture Editing by Magnus Bartlett
Production & printing supervision by Twin Age Ltd.
Captions by Jill Trew
Jacket & book design by Margaret Ng

Printed in China

Star Ferry

1989

A Star Ferry chases a vehicular ferry bound for Hung Hom in Victoria Harbour. Photographed from the Peak with a long lens, the two ferries are moving through a spectacular beam of light emanating from the massive golden buildings at the China Ferry Terminal in Yau Ma Tei.

FOREWORD

 I am glad that Keith Macgregor was out and about while I was too forgetful to carry a camera or was too preoccupied to realise that history was being built and destroyed before my eyes! All I have of those days of arrival in Hong Kong forty years ago, are things which stand out in the memory and a few scrappy black and white snaps: children standing in line to receive their vitamins, huts with thatched roofs, a Governor wearing a safari suit and trilby hat on a rural visit, myself on a bicycle riding through the vegetable farms. Hong Kong was small, poor and alone, anxiously remembering the anguish of war and still suffering its legacy, unable to see the greater picture, the good fortune around the corner. It seems almost impossible to think that one of my tasks in those days was to look after a stockpile of firewood, corned beef, rice and soya beans, in case we were besieged!

In the late sixties I painted a picture in rural Hong Kong of a broad valley, golden with ripening paddy. Now, except for the hobby of a few, not a grain of rice is grown in Hong Kong. My house for many years was on a wooded island, whose foreshore was once littered with the stone adzes of prehistoric Hong Kong and it stood at the entrance to a small market town. It is now a lonely outpost of a small city of two hundred and fifty thousand.

BY SIR DAVID AKERS-JONES

Like Keith, one of my most easily recalled memories is of sails. Sampans with scraps of sail helping their strenuous row across the harbour, boats with jib-like sails rigged at bow and stern, fishing as they were blown down wind, huge junks with great high round storehouses beating and hauling across the bay, junks with loads of bricks clawing their way up river, a few junks lazily taking the short cut through the harbour, working against the tide, their crew incurious of the grey city and the high mountains slowly drifting past.

That grey city is now a glitter of glass and light. The arcaded shipping offices with their flagpoles and rococo have long gone and in their place huge gold, green, blue, glass-walled towers face the harbour, where shivering in the winter of 1840, Captain Elliott literally took the law into his hands and moved ashore, thereby creating the Colony.

If you walk westwards now, away from the marble arcades and grand offices you will still find the shopfronts of tea and rice merchants, tin beaters, traditional medicine, real and fake antiques, while eastwards are the colourful, provocative, beckoning signs crowding one another for attention, even blotting out the sky, of bars and nightclubs. South, walk steeply up the hill past the alleyways of flower sellers to the Peak, and you pass through a forest of ferns and a jungle of trees, home of the porcupine, pangolin and barking deer.

From the Peak, the first magical look at the circle of mountains and sea of islands. North to the mainland and on a

PREVIOUS PAGE
Chek Lap Kok
1970

Mainland Chinese junks on a becalmed sea near Castle Peak opposite Chek Lap Kok, now the site of the new airport. These delicate, butterfly-like sailing craft are in fact working cargo boats which carry building materials, timber and other goods down the coast of China from Shantou and Xiamen (formerly known to the West as Swatow and Amoy) and up the Pearl River to Guangzhou (Canton). Chinese sailing junks were not uncommon in Hong Kong waters in the 1970s when this picture was taken, but by the mid 1980s they were a rarity, and now, sadly, have all but disappeared.

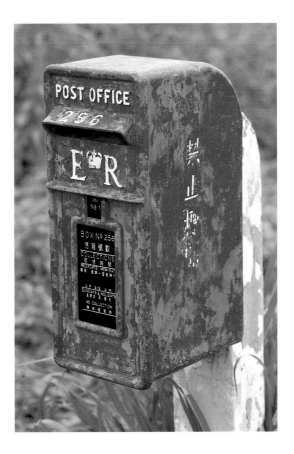

clear day, ridge upon ridge of mountains fading into the far horizon. South, the islands humped against the glittering sunpath and in the distance, hanging in the sky. Gone from the sea are the sails; bulk carriers, container ships, coasters, barges, row upon row, crowd the anchorages; catamarans, jet and hover ferries trace white arrows through the water, hurrying to and from the great populations of China.

Twenty years ago if you stood on the hills on the northern boundary of Hong Kong you looked across a muddy river to a silent world of farmers moving in distant fields; now if you stood on that same spot you would see that the tall towers of a great city of three million people have marched to the border and that both sides of the border look very much the same.

Hong Kong has always been Chinese. It seems to me now, at the end of its colonial life, that a hundred and sixty years have been merely a strand in the slow drift of history, a passing interlude, an intrusion and that the great buildings, the ships, the port, the airport, the great power stations, are not simply a monument to empire but a creation of the people of Hong Kong. All who have lived here and loved Hong Kong, have been part of a great endeavour which has made this wonderful place.

What a joy it is that we now have this thoughtful collection, one man's observation, to bring to life and sharpen our memory and to whet the appetite of those who have yet to come, of the sea, mountains, city, the place and its people and even its little things like letterboxes.

Letterboxes

1975 & 1994

Hong Kong has a very reliable, efficient postal service, which handled
1.2 billion items of mail in 1995. The wall of boxes was near Lau Fau Shan
and the Royal Mail one near Fanling. Boxes like this will disappear after the
handover and are already collectors' items.

CONTENTS

Hei Ling Chau

1973

Pulling in the nets at Hei Ling Chau, a small island
which lies to the southeast of Lantau. Fishing is very
much a family affair in Hong Kong and every
member of the family, old and young, is involved.

INTRODUCTION

"Macgregor House"
44 Foochow Road, Shanghai
Occupied on 31st March, 1937
by
Caldbeck, Macgregor & Co., Ltd.
Wine and Spirit Merchants
Established 1864

My great-grandfather John Macgregor was the younger son of a Scottish crofter family in Callander, Central Scotland, and was forced, because of the primogeniture inheritance laws in Scotland, to seek his fortune elsewhere. He joined the merchant navy in Glasgow and headed East to China. After a few voyages there he set up in business for himself, going into the wine and spirits trade in 1864, the same year which saw the foundation of the Hongkong and Shanghai Banking Corporation. These were turbulent times in China with the Ching dynasty in its death throes and foreigners still experiencing the aftermath of the Taiping rebellion. However the Suez Canal opened in 1869 and the telegraph reached Hong Kong and Shanghai in 1870 which gave a huge boost to China Coast traders.

John Macgregor remained in Shanghai but branches of Caldbeck Macgregor and Co. Ltd., as the company was then known, opened in Hong Kong, Tien Tsin, Penang, Kuala Lumpur and Ipoh. He was an avid horse racing enthusiast and built up a large stable which he raced all over China, usually riding his horses himself. He retired to Kent in the 1890s leaving the business to his sons, Norman and Jack, my grandfather, who took over the firm at the very young age of 25. He moved to Hong Kong and met Dorothy Shelton Hooper who was born in Hong Kong and was the daughter of the first manager of Sir Paul Chater's Hong Kong Land Investment Company. They were married in St John's Cathedral in 1911, where I was also married exactly 60 years later. My father, Robin was born in 1916 just before my grandfather was

LEFT
Hong Kong from Glenealy
1879

The exquisite pencil and watercolour is by Constance
Gordon Cumming (1837-1924). She arrived in Hong Kong on
Christmas Day 1878 and her subsequent experiences in the East
are described in her book "Wanderings in China". This was
painted at Glenealy, the property of the mercantile house of
Gibb Livingstone and Co.

*(courtesy of Martyn Gregory © and the collection of
Mr. and Mrs. Peter Thompson of Hong Kong)*

gassed in Normandy while serving as an officer on the Somme in the Great War. He survived and after a year in a German prisoner of war camp returned to Hong Kong to resume running the firm, which involved moving back and forth between Hong Kong and Shanghai. He also travelled to London from Hong Kong many times on the Trans-Siberian railway to visit his wife and sons who were at schools in England.

My mother, Imogen Newman, was born in Shanghai. Her father was a solicitor and her mother a leading light in Shanghai amateur dramatic life. She and her elder sister Marylou were two very pretty young ladies and were in great demand in the vibrant and hectic pre-war social life of Shanghai. My father met her in 1938 and they became engaged in 1940 when my mother was only 18. In 1941, as war had broken out with Germany my father went to Calcutta to enlist in the British army. My mother followed three months later and on

the stopover in Hong Kong was joined by my grandparents who then sailed with her to Calcutta for the wedding. Fortunately my grandmother did not travel light as while the wedding was taking place in Calcutta both Shanghai and Hong Kong fell to the Japanese. Their war was consequently spent in India in relative comfort compared with the rest of their family members who were not so fortunate and were incarcerated in various Japanese prisoner of war camps.

I came on the scene in Bangalore in 1946. Six months later at Christmas of the same year I landed in Hong Kong from a troop ship in the arms of my mother. If I had been old enough to use a camera then I would have recorded a small city in disarray trying to pick it itself up after a cruel Japanese occupation which had forced half of the pre-war population back to China. The city was in a sorry state and very short of food and fuel. Even the Peninsula Hotel was an army barracks. My grandfather's house on Barker

Kowloon-Canton Railway Terminal
1976

Completed in 1915, the station was the terminus for Hong Kong's rail link with the interior of China. From the 1930s this was connected to the Trans-Siberian Railway, allowing those who wished to avoid the six-week steamer trip from Hong Kong to England to reach Victoria station in London just 18 days from Hong Kong. The station was demolished in 1978. Behind the station are the YMCA, the Peninsula and Sheraton Hotels.

Road was a ruin with most of its woodwork stripped to provide fuel for the desperate people of Hong Kong during the occupation. But it was not long before these same people were back on their feet again. However on the mainland things were much worse. China was in the midst of a devastating civil war following straight after the horrors of the Japanese invasion. Hong Kong was about to experience the consequences of this in the form of a huge influx of refugees both immediately after the war and more so after 1949.

Like many other British and Chinese businessmen my grandfather's overriding concern was to rebuild his shattered and bankrupted business. He did this remarkably quickly with the help of the Hongkong and Shanghai Bank. He even opened a branch in Tokyo in 1947. My father was sent to Kuala Lumpur to reopen the business there but in 1948 with things not looking too hopeful for western companies in China a decision was made to expand, not in Asia but into Africa. With hindsight this was, of course, unfortunate as Asia was and is the place to be. It did mean, however, that we spent ten happy years in the beautiful country of Kenya.

On returning to Hong Kong to live in 1959 we found a very different place: a population which had grown from 1.5 million in 1947 to 3 million, a virtually autonomous territory administratively and financially and a powerful Chinese élite on equal terms with British merchants in all spheres of public life. An economic miracle

was taking place with Hong Kong now a manufacturer of textiles, enamelware, plastics and later, consumer electronics. My own memories of it are limited as I was only here for eight weeks a year, two years out of three. In this short time away from school in England I was much too preoccupied with the normal pursuits of the average expatriate teenager: girls, beaches, parties and watersports. If I had had then my present interests I would have photographed a city which still had many of its grand Victorian buildings, a New Territories where age-old methods of farming and village life remained untouched by the rapid changes occurring in the urban areas. Sha Tin for example was still a verdant valley of rice paddies and Sai Kung looked little different from remote areas of China.

On my 21st birthday my parents gave me a Pentax, my first serious camera. From that day, unbeknownst to me, my life was set. After leaving Oxford University, on the urging of an adventurous mother of a friend, I joined a bus going overland from London to Kathmandu in Nepal. Armed with my new camera, a few rolls of film, a sleeping bag and £120 in traveller's cheques we set off to India in our totally inadequate vehicle (it broke down 6 times before reaching Teheran!) It was on this trip that the seeds of my passion for travel photography were sown. After crossing the Bosphorus into Asia it required very strong discipline not to use all of my meagre supply of film in the first few days.

Central and Victoria Harbour
1974

The aerial shot was taken from a helicopter hovering above Mount Nicholson. Victoria Peak and Mount Gough, dotted with magnificently located houses and complexes of flats, are to the left. Below, Central is already dominated by a scattering of high-rise blocks, notably the 52-storey Connaught Centre which at that time was almost twice the size of its neighbours. The emerald patch of the Hong Kong Cricket Club ground can be clearly seen.

1948

1970

The Harbour
1998

The phenomenal changes since 1970 are obvious. Hong Kong has grown into a sophisticated international city with architecture to rival anywhere in the world. Across the harbour in Kowloon is where the greatest changes are now taking place. One can already seen the large reclamation project of Yau Ma Tei (centre left) and now that the airport is at Chek Lap Kok all height restrictions on the Kowloon peninsula will be removed.

PREVIOUS PAGES
The Harbour and City
1948

This photograph was taken by Mee Cheung of Ice House Street. It shows clearly the Hong Kong and Shanghai Bank, the cricket ground and the naval dockyard. Government House is with its newly acquired tower, courtesy of General Isogai, the Japanese governor during the occupation.

PREVIOUS PAGES BOTTOM
The Harbour and City
1970

The north shore of Hong Kong Island, Victoria Harbour, and Kowloon with the New Territories beyond, seen from Pollock's Path on the eastern side of the Peak. This magnificent view has acted as a yardstick for tracing Hong Kong's rapid development over the past 30 years. In Central, Gammon House (now renamed Bank of America Building) was half built, while the Hong Kong Hilton and Mandarin Hotel were already open.
In the foreground on the far right is the site of the Chief Justice's House which had been destroyed in the Second World War and was rumoured to be haunted. It was not redeveloped until the late 1980s.

The journey lasted three months and ended with me in hospital in Hong Kong laid up with severe amoebic hepatitis. After a slow recovery my long-suffering parents, who had been dead against the bus trip in the first place, felt that I needed to learn about life and earn my own living, so I was dispatched off to New York where I joined J.E. Seagram as a management

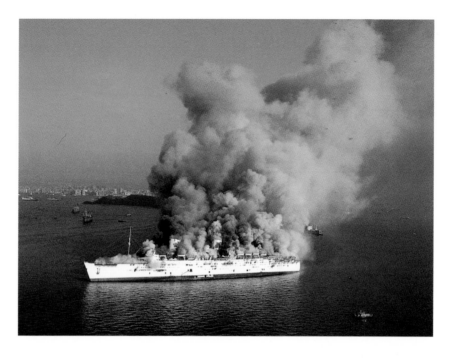

trainee. It was there that I learnt to print my own negatives in the cramped confines of my minuscule West Side apartment. This must be the moment when many photographers become truly hooked. I look back at both the results of my photographic efforts on the bus trip and my early attempts at print making with some amusement but the wonder of that first print remains locked in my memory.

The sad and untimely death of my father in 1969 brought me unexpectedly back to Hong Kong. I had had no intention prior to this of living here but my brief encounter with corporate life in New York had convinced me that it should be avoided at all costs. In truth I had no idea what I wanted to do. Photography as a profession had not even occurred to me. It was only when I accompanied my mother to Angkor Wat in Cambodia in 1970 that I began to consider it seriously. I was carried away by the powerful beauty of that fascinating ancient city buried in the jungle and I was also inspired there by the courteous and unselfish encouragement and help given to me by a Hungarian American photographer I met there named Bela Kalman. Back in Hong Kong our next door neighbour was the renowned Time Life photographer, Larry Burrows who also inspired me and urged me to go ahead. His death later in Cambodia was a tragic loss to all who knew him.

I began by photographing children and doing family portraits. This is an excellent discipline for a new boy in the profession and gave me the chance to learn to be a good printmaker and at the same time earn a very reasonable living. I was able then to venture into corporate and advertising, industrial and aerial photography and most importantly some travel assignments came my way. I also began photographing Hong Kong whenever I had the time.

In 1974 a leading hotel agreed to sponsor an exhibition of my photographs of Hong Kong and Indonesia. It was there

RMS Queen Elizabeth I

1972

The fire totally destroyed the 83,675-ton luxury liner, the largest passenger vessel ever built, and the wreckage sank into the depths of the Harbour where she has remained ever since. Launched by Cunard in 1938, for 30 years she was the most opulent of liners in the great era of transatlantic sea travel. After her last passenger voyage in 1968, she was bought by Hong Kong shipping magnate C.Y. Tung (father of Hong Kong's first post-1997 chief executive) and was moved to Hong Kong in 1970 to be fitted out as a floating university. Her new name, 'Seawise University', a pun on the name of her owner, was being painted on the bow at the time of the fire.

Convention and Exhibition Centre

1997

The new extension to the Convention and Exhibition Centre is clearly visible in this dusk view from the Peak. The complex, costing $4.8 Billion was the venue of the official handover ceremony marking the end of 156 years of British colonial rule. It was designed by Wong and Ouyang of Hong Kong and Skidmore, Owings and Merrill of Chicago.

Lantau Flowers

1997

Let us hope that we will continue to be able to see scenes
like this in Lantau now that the airport road link has opened
up the island to massive potential development.

RIGHT

The Lantau Link, Tsing Ma Bridge

1998

This bridge is the key element in the 34 kilometre
direct road and rail network leading to Hong Kong
International Airport at Chek Lap Kok.
At 2.2 km the bridge will be the world's longest
combined road and rail suspension bridge.
The main span is a staggering 1,377 metres.
The total length of the 160,000 km suspension
cable wire is enough to circle the world four times.
The new airport opened on July 6, 1998.

Lai Chi Wo Village

1997

This almost perfectly preserved walled village lies on the west side of Crooked Harbour
(Kat O Hoi) in the North East part of the Territories, bordering China.

RIGHT

Central and the Peak

1974

Photographed from above Mt. Nicholson in a helicopter, this view of
Central and the Peak shows Jardine House as the tallest building in the city.
The cricket pitch can be seen clearly in front.

Happy Valley

1975 & 1994

As this was the only piece of flat land on the island it was chosen to be the site of the racecourse. Known in Chinese as Wong Nei Chong or "Yellow mud stream", it was a noxious, unhealthy place full of swamps and rice fields. It was drained in 1844 and the first race meeting was on December 17, 1846. The racecourse is still there, but what a far cry from those days! These two photographs show the huge developments which have taken place in a mere 19 years.

香港 **HONG KONG** *Dragon boat*

that I met Geoff Cloke, the managing director of Mandarin Publishers, Paul Hamlyn's production company here. Geoff suggested that we publish the Hong Kong pictures in the form of a wall calendar which we would sell to corporate clients. So we created Cameraman Ltd. and the 1975 and 1976 wall calendars were the result. The partnership did not work out but I kept the calendar concept going, and the 1998 edition will be my 24th in succession.

Some years later I was persuaded by friends to try and do something to upgrade the very poor standard of postcards in Hong Kong. After a slow start this took off and it now gives me a huge amount of satisfaction to know that this year over two and a half million people all over the world will receive one of my postcards through their letter boxes.

I gradually ceased to do corporate or advertising work in the early '80s as a result of an increasing involvement in a business, started with my wife, selling as many of the most beautiful objets d'art, antiques, textiles and furniture as we could find in Asia. This grew so fast and took up so much of my time that it was difficult to do much else. The calendars and postcards continued, however, and are what have kept me in photography.

This book is a result of 27 years of searching the length and breadth of Hong Kong for the types of photograph that suit those mediums. It has been an exhilarating task in a place which never ceases to surprise and fascinate. Editing the thousands of photographs has been an extraordinary undertaking but once a theme had been established, that of a journey round the whole territory from Central to the border with China, it became much easier. Sifting through all the early photographs has opened up a flood of memories. For example, the shot of the cricket ground in Chater Road reminds me of the wonderful afternoons spent there as a schoolboy. I can still feel the butterflies in my stomach as I pounded in to bowl against the local Hong Kong schoolboy cricket team. Those of the Hong Kong Club take me back to the all too few times I was taken there to lunch by my grandfather and father as a young lad. The views from our flat in Headland Road (pages 60 and 61) are particularly poignant because this is where I lived from 1959 till when I was married in 1971 and where I returned from 1989 to 1992 before I went to live in London. To start and finish up one's life in Hong Kong with a view like this, which has hardly changed in the intervening years, is remarkable

A city in constant movement
1978

Shot at slow speeds to convey the movement and excitement of this extraordinary city, the photograph above is of dragon boat racing in Aberdeen and to the left is Tai Yuen Street, Wanchai, where hawkers sell everything from fresh fruit and vegetables to T-shirts, nightdresses, haberdashery and hardware. This street was actually a thoroughfare, and every time a vehicle came down it, the whole market had to move aside.

considering the enormous changes which have taken place everywhere else. I am truly fortunate.

Hong Kong is a place whose people I have grown to love and respect, whose rhythms and colours intoxicate. It is also a place which sometimes bewilders and frustrates. Like most long-term residents here I suspect that we continually wish to escape from it but within weeks or days we hunger to return. The moment when the aeroplane touches down at Kai Tak one is carried away by a feeling of excitement and anticipation. One can sense the buzz in the air before reaching Immigration. Hong Kong is truly alive and this above all is what must be preserved in the future which lies ahead. Although I now live in London, I hope to return again and again to continue to record the life and times of this remarkable city to which I owe so much. This is my tribute to Hong Kong and its hard-working wonderful people. Long may it and they continue to prosper and flourish.

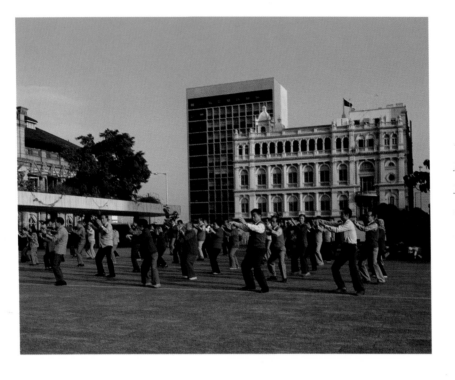

Old Hong Kong Club building

1978

The elegant colonnaded Hong Kong Club, which was founded in 1844 and moved here in 1897, was demolished in 1981 to make way for a high-rise building, which houses the club in a spacious, modern setting, and also yields substantial rental income from the many floors of offices above. Nonetheless, there are still those in Hong Kong who regret the demise of Central's last remaining example of Victorian colonial architecture. In the fore-ground early risers practise tai-chi, the traditional Chinese slow-motion form of callisthenics. Early in the morning one can see men and women of all ages throughout Hong Kong working through a series of movements with almost balletic grace.

PS. I have thought about producing this book for fifteen years. It is thanks to a few good friends and especially Magnus Bartlett, my old colleague, that it has finally happened. He undertook the exhausting task of editing thousands of my photographs and refusing to listen to my pleas, such as "Oh, you must pick that one; I remember it so clearly and it is one of my favourites".

I also wish to thank all who have worked with me over the years: Henry Lam and Ivan Lau, my two long-suffering assistants; Moby Lau, the excellent printer of my calendars and cards; Felicity Hunt, Edna Soriano and Gail Hung who ran Cameraman Ltd while I was preoccupied with Banyan Tree and all the wonderful staff of Banyan Tree.

I also want to thank my designer, Margaret Ng who has worked above and beyond the call of duty to get the book to print in time and Jill Trew who has been tireless with the captions.

Above all I want to thank the people of Hong Kong who have created this extraordinary, wonderful city.

The Hong Kong Cricket Club

1975

Just before the club moved to the wider open spaces of Wong Nei Chong Gap in
June 1975. Surprisingly, given the pace of change in this part of town, the three blocks
overlooking the ground are still standing in 1997: on the left is the old Bank of China
Building; in the centre is Prince's Building, an office and shopping block ; on the right is
the Mandarin Hotel, built by the Hong Kong Land Company in 1963, and since then
consistently listed amongst the world's best hotels.

THE ISLAND

Central
1996

From the roof of the YMCA in Kowloon in dramatic early morning light which highlights the Hongkong and Shanghai Bank on the left, Jardine House in the centre and the towers of Exchange Square to the right. On the Peak the silhouette of the new Peak Tower building, completed in 1996, can be seen. The Clock Tower, built in 1916, provides an interesting architectural contrast in the foreground.

RIGHT
Central
1996

This shot of the glittering lights of Central was taken in 1996 with a 60-second exposure from the Tsim Sha Tsui waterfront in front of the Cultural Centre. It would surely be hard to better this easily accessible spot for photographing Central's stunning skyline. To the right of the Bank of China is Citibank Tower, the Furama Hotel with its clearly distinguishable revolving restaurant, the Ritz Carlton, and the Hongkong Bank. The Bank of America Building is on the left of the China Bank.

PREVIOUS PAGE
The south side of the Island

This view from the Matilda Hospital on Mount Kellett Road encompasses, from right to left, the fishing port of Aberdeen with the island of Ap Lei Chau, Shum Wan, Wong Chuk Hang, Shouson Hill and on to Deep Water Bay, Repulse Bay and in the far distance the Stanley Peninsula. Lamma Island is on the far right of the picture.

Kennedy Town

1977

A typical old building in Eastern Street, Kennedy Town. Almost all these low-rise balconied
blocks have been replaced by highrise constructions.

LEFT
Central

1998

Central's most prominent buildings shot from the roof of the Tsim Sha Tsui YMCA at dawn.
The old clock tower and the roof of the Cultural Centre are in the foreground. On the far left
is the stunning Bank of China designed by I. M. Pei and on the right is the new 80 storey
"The Center", the lights of which change colour every few seconds after dusk.

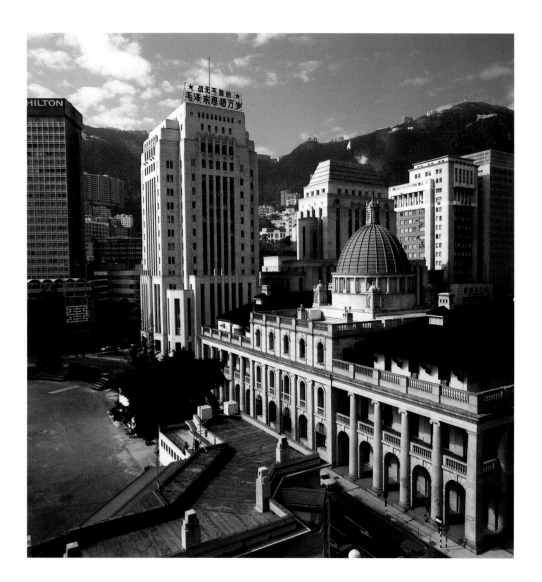

Central

1972 & 1995

The view from the old Hong Kong Club, across to the Supreme Court building. Opened in 1912 by the Governor, Sir Frederick Lugard, the granite building boasts Ionic columns, balustrades and arches reminiscent of late Victorian architecture in Britain. The building was designed by Webb and Bell who were also architects of the facade of Buckingham Palace. The Supreme Court moved out in 1983, when it became the home of the Legislative Council. Beyond it is the old China Bank building, which served for many years as a control centre for China's financial affairs in Hong Kong, and also for Beijing's political and diplomatic activities. To its right is the old Hongkong and Shanghai Bank building, built in the 1930s and demolished to make way for Norman Foster's new building in 1985. Further right is the Standard Chartered Bank building. On the far left is the Hong Kong Hilton, and in the foreground the Hong Kong Cricket Club - all of which have now gone. On page 25 is The Legislative Council building, now dwarfed by the new Hong Kong and Shanghai Bank.

Douglas Castle

1995

Now called University Hall, in an eerie light that emphasized the building's neo-gothic
features. Built in 1861 on a hill in Pokfulam by a Hong Kong shipping magnate,
John Douglas Lapraic, the odd mix of gothic and colonial styles, with turrets, battlements
and colonial arched balconies is strangely imposing. It was sold to the Société des
Missions Etrangères de Paris in 1894, who renamed it Nazareth House.
The French monks added a chapel and crypt, and stayed there until 1954 when it
was sold to the University of Hong Kong and became a student hall of residence.

LEFT

The old Post Office

1977

Opened in 1912 but sadly demolished in 1978 to make way for an undistinguished
commercial building called World Wide House.

The Bank of China

1996

Designed by brilliant Chinese American architect I.M.Pei, and completed in 1987, the 70-storey building stands at night like an almost transparent gossamer wing of a butterfly. With its series of dramatic triangular prisms, topped by twin masts, the building forcefully creates the commanding impact that the Bank of China required from its chosen architect.

RIGHT
Lippo Centre

Taken from a small observation tower in the middle of Hong Kong Park, this shot shows some of Hong Kong's best architecture against a sky of pastel blues and pinks. Citibank Tower is to the left, with the lower floors of the Bank of China next to it, and the Lippo Centre (formerly the Bond Centre) dominating on the right. Designed by eminent American architect Paul Rudolph, and opened in 1988, the light from the many facets of the Centre's two hexagonal towers provides particular visual interest.

Victoria Harbour
1998

Victoria Harbour from Lugard Road, the narrow road circling the Peak, offering a different, but equally magnificent view every few yards. Pictures from up here need updating twice a year because land reclamation and the pace of building make the scene change so rapidly. This is rightly considered to be one of the most exciting night views in the world.

Novice ballet dancers

1990

Novice ballet dancers at Jean Wong's School of Ballet. Ms Wong's school, the best known in the territory, has produced some fine international stars including dancers for London's Royal Ballet Company.

LEFT
Smiling Faces

The casual visitor to Hong Kong whose only experience of its people might be of the shopkeepers and taxi drivers of Tsim Sha Tsui could easily be misled into believing that it is an unfriendly and aggressive place. This is far from the truth; with a little effort and understanding he will find a genuine and friendly response and many a warm smile will greet him.

Wanchai
1995

It seems extraordinary that, despite new construction techniques, the use of traditional bamboo scaffolding is still standard practice in Hong Kong. The unsung heroes of the construction industry who create these vast, apparently flimsy frames seem oblivious to danger as they sit, often without harnesses, as high as 60 storeys up a building, lashing together the poles. One recent statistic claims that some three million pieces of bamboo are tied together around newly constructed, or disappearing buildings every year in Hong Kong.

OVERLEAF
Central from Pacific Place
1990

This staggering sunset appeared quite unexpectedly. No filters were used. The shot captures the Bank of China and several other buildings at an unusual angle. The Hilton's floodlit rooftop tennis court is clearly visible on the left. The hotel has since been demolished, making way for a larger building dedicated to offices which will yield even greater profits for its owners than the Hilton has over the past twenty years.

Harbour fishing

1980

Fishing outside the Royal Hong Kong Yacht Club. Even in those days the harbour did not appear to be the cleanest of places and one has to wonder about the condition of the catch from these waters. This might explain why a scene like this would be very rare today.

Western Harbour

1993

A cruise liner glides through shimmering water at sunset, having
just left the Ocean Terminal on the right, and the western harbour is
dotted with ships waiting to load or unload their goods.

Chinese Opera

Opera performances in specially erected 'matshed' theatres are often an integral part of local festivals. Traditional Cantonese opera is very much alive in Hong Kong, enjoyed by the younger generation as well as by their parents and grandparents. It depends heavily on colour and theatrical effects for its impact. Traditionally, scenery was not used beyond a plain wooden chair or table, everything else was supplied by the imagination. These days more realistic sets are common, but the performer still dominates the stage. Actors specialize in certain roles, which they continue to play throughout their careers. Singing is done in a characteristic falsetto voice that takes many years to perfect. Although it may sound harsh, it can still be highly expressive. In the past only men could become actors, but today all roles are unisex, depending on the talent of the individual. There are some 500 professional singers, actors and acrobats working in the profession augmented by visiting troupes from different regions of China.

Showtime

1995

Pupils from Jean Wong's junior ballet school put on a New Year
performance at Tai Koo Plaza.

RIGHT
Causeway Bay & the Typhoon Shelter

1994

On the island this is the busiest and most popular place for shopping.
It hardly sleeps, with shops staying open late into the night. The entrance
to the Cross Harbour Tunnel is on the right; an average of 125,650 vehicles
cross the harbour through it every day. The new buildings of the reclaimed
Wanchai North are on the far right.

Chinese New Year Fireworks
1996

Fireworks over Causeway Bay, to celebrate Chinese
New Year. Supported generously by the private sector,
Hong Kong has developed a reputation for putting on some
of the world's most extravagant and spectacular displays.
That being planned for the handover on July 1st will be the
greatest of all time.

OVERLEAF & PAGES 48-49
Trams in Johnston Road, Wanchai
1984

Hong Kong's tram service began in 1904 and by 1912
double-decker cars were in use, although it was not until
1925 that the roofs were enclosed to protect passengers
from scorching sun and heavy downpours. Today the trams
continue to provide a fascinating and inexpensive, if rather
slow, ride along 30 kilometres of Hong Kong's busiest
roads. Over the years the traditional green colour of the
trams has given way to the brilliant multi-coloured palate of
advertisers. The first advertisements were displayed on
small panels which were sold to individual advertisers, but
more recently the whole body of a tram has been used as a
promotional base for selling a myriad of items sought by the
Hong Kong consumer - just about anything from computers
and portable phones to ginseng, insect repellent, or
noodles. Standards of design and creativity are constantly
improving, and today's trams are probably the largest, most
inventive collection of moving billboards in the world.

Moon Festival

1992

Lanterns and flowers on sale in Lockhart Road in readiness for the Moon or Mid-Autumn Festival. Essential to the celebrations are paper lanterns, produced mainly in China, in an eclectic mix of traditional and modern designs that can feature anything from a Chinese lion or mythical horse to a jet or a gaudily-coloured tank. The proprietor in this picture adds to the charm of the scene by wearing traditional Chinese dress - a rare sight in Hong Kong these days.

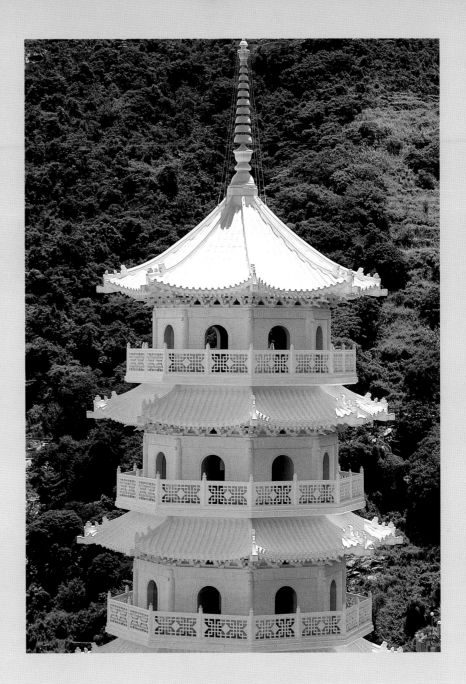

Tiger Balm Gardens Pagoda

Built in 1935, funded by the wealthy Chinese philanthropist Aw Boon Haw who made his fortune out of Tiger Balm, a famous cure-all which relieves asthma, sore throats, insect bites and much else.

LEFT

Causeway Bay

1996

From Sir Cecil's Ride–a footpath which winds round Mount Butler, said to be a favourite spot of the very able governor, Sir Cecil Clementi, who took up the post in 1925. Sir Cecil and Lady Penelope loved Hong Kong, and, on reluctantly leaving in 1930, said they 'would have stayed here rather than anywhere else in the world.' Clearly the view from the path has completely changed since then, but it still offers an excellent vantage point and a fine walk.

Shau Kei Wan Typhoon Shelter

1994

Small sampans share this shelter with larger ocean-going fishing vessels. This particular
spot has since been filled in, and the boats have been moved further into the harbour.

RIGHT
Shau Kei Wan

1996

The bustle of the Kam Wa Street market is captured with a long lens and a slow speed.
This is where the tramway ends and the trams turn full circle and start their long journey
back to Kennedy Town, which is the western terminus of the system.

Wanchai Market

1980s

Chinese vegetables for sale in Wanchai Market. Hong Kong's markets never cease to delight with their enticing array of fresh fruit and vegetables and their boisterous stall-holders. The tradition of buying food fresh each day is deeply entrenched in the Hong Kong lifestyle, and markets continue to hold their own in the war against convenience shopping in supermarkets. Hong Kong people also consume a massive quantity of oranges, often served at the end of a meal.

FAR RIGHT

Ta Kwu Ling

1996

Harvesting vegetables in the closed area on the border with China, across which workers come every day to tend the high-quality produce in this area, replacing Hong Kong's own farm labourers who have been attracted away by better-paid work in other industries. The vegetables, which are grown without heavy use of chemicals, command a higher price than those imported from China, and go straight to the tables of Hong Kong's top hotels.

Shek O

1996

Shek O Headland, taken from just under D'Aguilar Peak. It seems extraordinary to find
this magnificent, wild coastline and rough scrubby vegetation so near an urban centre.
The headland itself has changed little over the past quarter century, although more sand
has been added to Shek O Beach which is packed with sunbathers at weekends. Beyond is
the Tat Hong Channel, with the island of Tung Lung in the distance; the little island in the
foreground is Ng Fan Chau.

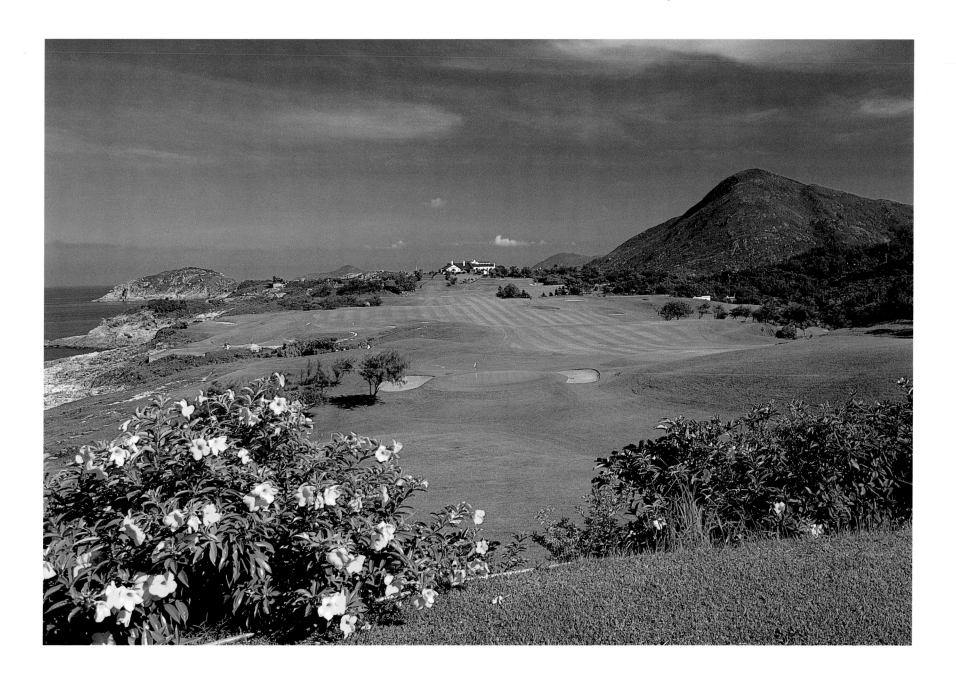

Shek O Golf and Country Club

1996

This exclusive private club has occupied one of the most beautiful corners of Hong Kong
for some seventy years.

Tai Tam Bay

1996

This view from Shek O Peninsula encompasses Tai Tam Bay and the residential development of Red Hill, with Stanley Peninsula stretching into the distance.

LEFT
Stanley Bay

1980

Named after Lord Stanley, Secretary of State for the Colonies, this was an established village with some 2,000 inhabitants in 1841. A battery and fort were quickly established here and, in the 1930s, a new fort was built on the headland, with barracks, soldiers' and officers' quarters, a school, church and mess. The British army withdrew in 1994 leaving the magnificent site for property developers. Today, Stanley is predominantly a middle-class residential area, but somehow it has managed to keep something of a seaside village atmosphere, with its bustling market and narrow streets.

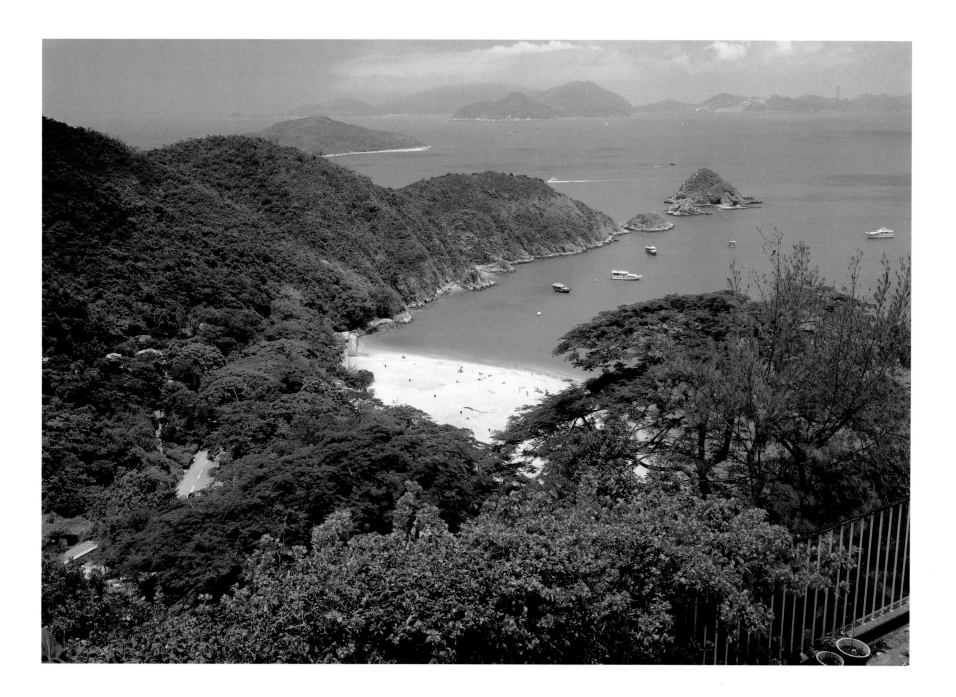

South Bay

1992 & 1976

This view over the bay and the Lamma Channel, supposedly one of the busiest shipping lanes in the world, has remained unchanged for years. The beach has been enlarged to increase the attraction of swimming here. It is a peaceful place although very popular in summer. The tranquil shot of two small sampans heading off to fish in the bay at dusk

Lido complex
1996

The gaudy but incredibly popular Lido complex, built by the Fung Ping Fan family, lies in front of the Life Guards Association on Repulse Bay Beach. Every morning, the Lido's concrete Buddhist garden, built in 1990, is flooded with visitors from Japan, Korea, Taiwan and Mainland China who come to photograph the Disneyland versions of figures from Chinese religion and mythology that ornament the site. On the previous page the three rams set against the sunset are messengers of the gods, while the goddess in the extravagantly-fringed head-dress is the sea goddess Tin Hau, the Queen of Heaven, and one of Hong Kong's most worshipped Taoist divinities. On this page is the serene figure of the Goddess of Mercy, Kwun Yum, who is loved and worshipped by Buddhists as well as Taoists.

PREVIOUS PAGE
Repulse Bay
1996

The sandy shallow bay got its name from the 19th-century pirate-chaser, HMS Repulse. Once a preferred picnic spot for the privileged, and accessible only by boat, it is now the easiest beach on the island to reach by public transport and tens of thousands flock here during the long hot months despite occasional scares about the cleanliness of the water. More sand was added in 1996 to increase beach capacity. Views from the expensive residential apartments behind the beach are spectacular - even by Hong Kong's high standards. The middle photograph on the right shows these apartments just before night falls.

The Repulse Bay Hotel

1978

This wonderful old hotel, which opened on New Year's Day in 1920, was best known for its gracious open verandah that looked across the bay, a favourite place for afternoon tea or dinner under twirling ceiling fans. The widespread public dismay when the hotel was torn down in 1982 for redevelopment led the owners, Hongkong and Shanghai Hotels, to incorporate a replica of the restaurant into the new complex, but inevitably the atmosphere is completely different.

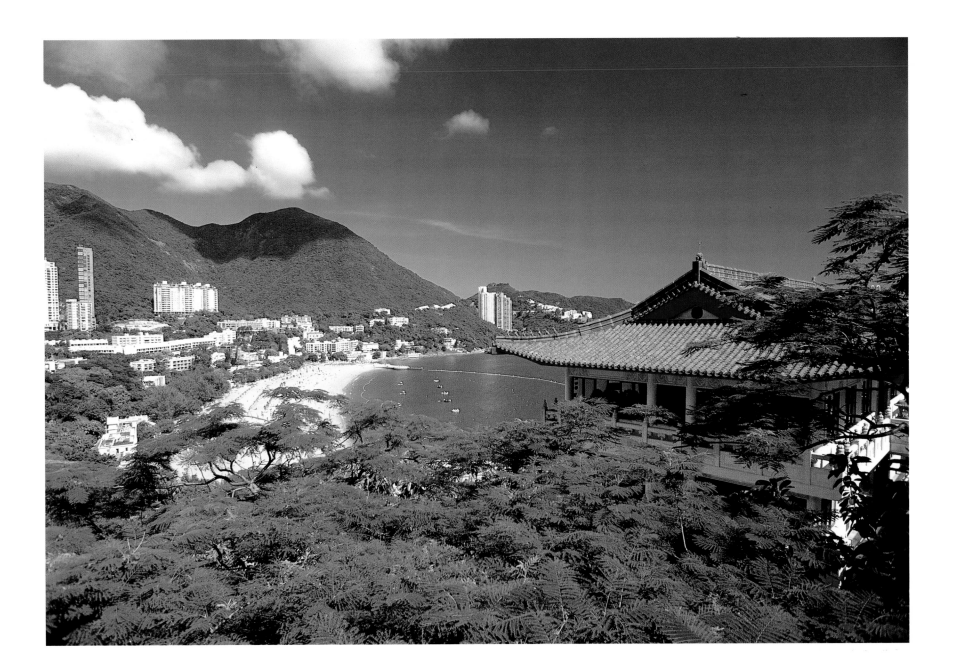

Repulse Bay

1996

The brilliant green roof of a luxurious old-style Chinese house frames Repulse Bay on a
glorious sunny day in July.

Fisherwoman
1986

Fisherwoman in a traditional Tanka hat, Aberdeen. These woven straw hats, with flattened crowns and turned down brims, are worn by both men and women in fishing communities throughout the region. They are made over the border in Guangdong Province.

LEFT
Sampan
1976

Sampan buzzing through Aberdeen Harbour. These small motorized boats still weave in and out of the larger vessels in the harbour, ferrying people and goods around, just as they did 20 years ago. The only change is in the style of the fishing boats behind - their traditional wooden junk-like hulls have been superseded by a sleeker and more efficient design.

RIGHT
Aberdeen
1984

Preparing wooden casks to hold fish landed from the boats. The boy chisels out Chinese characters in the wood, while his mother fills in the indented characters with red paint.

PREVIOUS PAGE
Deep Water Bay
1996

Luxury residential apartment blocks line Repulse Bay Road above the Bay. Island Road and its smaller houses and apartments hug the shoreline. Middle Island with its small yacht club is in the centre and through the gap one can see Repulse and South Bays with Headland Road above.

Aberdeen

1977

The busy fishing port with the island of Ap Lei Chau behind, seen from the air.
Ap Lei Chau has since undergone rapid development, and a large estate of
highrise public housing blocks now dominates the island's skyline. However,
the island's long-established boat building industry, visible in this picture, has
survived, and today wooden junks and other small craft are still being built
at the water's edge.

Aberdeen, Chinese New Year

1974

This large natural harbour has long been used by the Chinese. In the Ming Dynasty wood of the incense tree, which grew abundantly in Hong Kong, was shipped from here to Guangzhou. When the British arrived, the harbour was named after Lord Aberdeen, who was Foreign Secretary from 1841-1846. By 1860 it was chosen as the location for Hong Kong's first dock for ship repairs, with the Royal Navy its chief customer. Although its importance as a general port waned, the town continues to be a centre for commercial fishing and ship repairs.

Dragon Boat Races

1974

Aberdeen Harbour is one of the most exciting venues to watch Hong Kong's famous dragon boat races. The races are held throughout Hong Kong - as well as in Central and Southern China - to celebrate the Double Fifth (the fifth day of the fifth moon in the Chinese calendar). The long canoe-like boats, in which the paddlers sit two-abreast, are headed by magnificent dragon heads which are detached after the race and kept in local temples for the remainder of the year. The Chinese dragon is a beneficent creature, not the unpleasant character of European mythology, and has a wide mouth decorated with whiskers, and a beard which hides a shining pearl. The biggest dragon boats can be up to 100 feet long, with as many as 50 paddlers, a drummer who sets the pace, and an oarsman who stands at the stern and steers. It would be very difficult to take this shot today; the boats no longer race so closely together, and the races cover a longer distance.

Aberdeen, Chinese New Year

1996

At this time of year the majority of the fishing fleet returns home to celebrate the New Year
with their families, now living in apartments rather than on their boats as they did in the
past. As a result Aberdeen is jam packed and the sound of firecrackers is heard all over
the harbour even though they are officially banned.

Tam Kung Festival

1996

Fishing boats decorated to celebrate the Tam Kung Festival, ready to set out from Aberdeen to Shau Kei Wan Temple. Tam Kung is another god who appeals mostly to boat people and harbour lightermen because he is supposed to be able to control the weather. Besides calming storms he is also able to heal the sick by influencing their subconscious minds while asleep. The festival is usually held on the 8th day of the 4th moon. In 1998 this will be the 3rd of May.

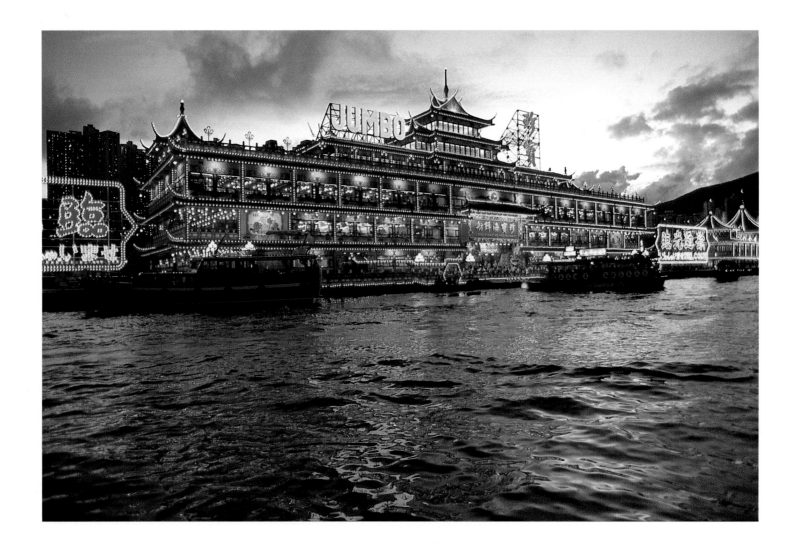

Aberdeen Harbour, Chinese New Year

1996

Aberdeen is home to Hong Kong's largest fishing fleet. Although many fishing families have
been rehoused in the blocks overlooking the harbour, others continue to live on their boats.
A trip through Aberdeen's congested typhoon shelter at night still gives a fascinating
glimpse into the life of Hong Kong's fishing families, much of it played out very publicly on
open deck. Although numbers of professional fishermen are declining, fishing remains an
important industry; 21,600 working fishermen on 4,800 fishing vessels were registered
in 1996. Three quarters of the fish landed in Hong Kong are caught by trawling.
The picture above shows the famous Jumbo Floating Restaurant moored in Shum Wan,
south Aberdeen.

KOWLOON

A Junk
1978

A junk heads straight for the camera, while I was on a boat in Victoria Harbour. These beautiful craft looked good from every angle and perspective.

RIGHT
Central and Kowloon
1998

Taken from the Peak, this shot of Central and Kowloon shows Exchange Square with the Outlying Islands Ferry Pier in front of it. On the left is the new 80 storey "The Center", the lights of which change colour every few seconds.

PREVIOUS PAGE
Tsim Sha Tsui Clock Tower
1996 & 1971

This is all that remains of the Kowloon-Canton Railway Terminal, demolished in 1978. The clock, installed in 1921, was beset with technical problems, and even now each of the four clock faces shows a slightly different time. Behind is the Hong Kong Cultural Centre complex, built on the site of the demolished railway station and opened in 1989. Dubbed 'the ski-slope' by locals, many have wondered how a building which would certainly provide those inside with one of the world's finest views came to be designed without windows.

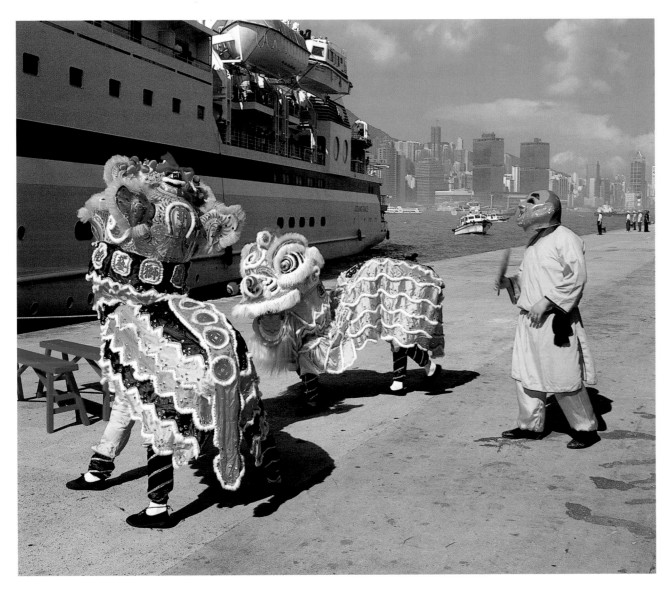

Lion Dances
1994

Lion dances welcome arriving cruise-ship passengers at Ocean Terminal. These boisterous, energetic dances, accompanied by rhythmic drums, gongs and clashing cymbals, are performed at a wide variety of propitious occasions in Hong Kong - anything from a small hospital fete or the official opening of a major new office block or hotel to a traditional Chinese festival. The Chinese for dancing lions *mo si* sounds similar to the words for 'no trouble', and thus the lions are helpful in securing a troublefree future.

LEFT
Ocean Terminal
1979

The Queen Elizabeth II and the SS Canberra lie alongside Ocean Terminal, the main berth for luxury cruise liners.

Peninsula Hotel

1996

The new extension of the Peninsula Hotel, with the dome of the Space Museum in front. One of the great old hotels of Asia, 'the Pen' opened in December 1928. It was here that the Governor of Hong Kong formally surrendered to the Japanese in 1941, after which it briefly became the Toa Hotel and the headquarters of the Japanese governor. Owners, Hongkong and Shanghai Hotels, restarted the hotel operation in 1946, and have continued to upgrade the property since then to maintain the Pen's position as the grande dame of Hong Kong's hotels. In 1994 the new tower opened and the hotel's room count increased from 210 to 300. Despite the recent appearance of many of the world's top hotel brand names in the territory, none can rival the fame or atmosphere of the Peninsula's gracious, high-ceilinged lobby, for so long one of 'the' places to meet in Asia. At the 1928 opening, an American visitor was heard to say: " I'd feel rich here if I hadn't a dime in my bag." The Sheraton Hotel is on the right and the YMCA, a comfortable hotel which belies the spartan image conjured up by its name, is on the left.

Nathan Road and Mong Kok

1994

The Golden Mile of Nathan Road and its side streets such as Peking Road are ablaze with colour at night. Shops stay open until the early hours. This is understandable when rents in this area reach dizzying heights. A money changer here is paying HK$110,000.00 (£8,800.00) per month for a space of 34.5 square feet! Nathan Road is Kowloon's main thoroughfare, and the heart of Hong Kong's retail life. It was named after Sir Matthew Nathan, Governor from 1904-1907, who had ambitiously hoped to build a road to Guangzhou and beyond. In fact, it never got further than Boundary Street on the edge of Kowloon. It is hard to reconcile a resident's description of the road in the 1920s as 'a lovely peaceful place, lined with large trees' with the present noisy, fumed-filled road thronging with shoppers from every corner of the world.

The man with the golden teeth

1994

This man was doing touch-up paintwork on the hull of the Queen Elizabeth II.
I was sitting in the lounge with the executive chef when his smiling face full of golden dental
work appeared at the window.

Shanghai Street

1986

A traditional herbal teashop on the corner of Shanghai Street and Public Square Street in Mong Kok. Sadly, this building has been demolished, but the business of selling herbal tea is still thriving in Hong Kong. The proprietors of this shop are still doing good business in their newer, grander premises.

Tin Hau Temple, Yau Ma Tei

1996

Buried amongst the anonymous-looking tenement blocks, this temple houses the sea goddess, who is also the Taoist Queen of Heaven. When the temple complex was built over 100 years ago, the sea was a few yards away, but reclamation has pushed the water back several blocks and buildings have cut off any sea view. The temple was carefully restored in the 1970s, keeping as much to the original materials and design as possible. These huge spiral coils of incense hanging from the roof represent a long-term offering, for some will burn for as long as two weeks. For around HK$100 you may have your name hung on to one of the coils.

Tin Hau Temple, Yau Ma Tei
1995

Built between 1870-1876, there are in fact
four temples dedicated to a great many
gods. There are three shelves with images
of the Tai Sui (the 60 gods of the year), one
god representing each year of the 60-year
cycle. Whatever the problem, the right god
to handle the difficulty can be found here.
Immediately to the left is the entrance to
Shea Tan, dedicated to the local community.

Tung Choi Street Market, Mong Kok

1994

This is the biggest of all Hong Kong street markets. All manner of merchandise can be
found here at very competitive prices, but it is clothes that provide the best bargains.
The other famous market is in Temple Street to the west of Nathan Road.

Wong Tai Sin Temple, Chinese New Year

Worshippers with joss sticks. Built in 1973, this is one of Hong Kong's
newest temples, and throughout the year attracts huge numbers who come
to give offerings of fruit and other food, burn joss sticks and to pray to the
gods. Both young and old from all sections of Hong Kong's community
worship here. Of all Hong Kong's gods, the Taoist Wong Tai Sin has the
best reputation for granting the wishes of devotees, particularly those
related to illness and horse racing tips. The temple is surrounded by
fortune tellers and stalls selling temple tack. There are more than 350
Chinese temples in the territory, 43 of which are managed by the
Chinese Temples Committee as public temples.

RIGHT
Hungry Ghost Festival

1984

A bustling scene in Kwun Tong where large-scale celebrations for the
festival are in full swing. During the festival the vast number of ghosts, or
disembodied spirits, that are believed to roam freely at this time of year,
need to be placated with gifts and with several nights of operatic shows.
The brilliantly coloured matshed theatre in the background is erected
specially to house these performances, and is removed at the end
of the festival.

Dried-food wholesale store

1996

A dried-food wholesale store in Kowloon City, stocked for
Chinese New Year with an impressive array of dried
sausages and fish, including abalone, fish skin, shark's fin,
shrimps, dried mushrooms and other delicacies. Some of
the prices are staggering: abalone, hanging in the centre of
the picture, is HK$3,600 a piece (around £280) and a catty
(0.67 kg) of birds' nests costs the same.

Village Children

A little girl lovingly tends to her brother. One often sees young children being responsible for their even younger siblings. Above left: This traditional means of carrying a baby is still quite widely used in Hong Kong.

FAR LEFT
Kau Wah Keng

1981

This old tile-roofed village lies nestled between the industrial concrete of Cheung Sha Wan and Lai Chi Kok and the vast container port of Kwai Chung. Amazingly it is still almost intact today, although negotiations are under way with a property developer to demolish it and build a huge residential estate of high rises.

Monkey God Festival

1984

At this festival in Sau Mau Ping a 'medium', empowered for the occasion with the supernatural abilities of the impish Monkey God, demonstrates the Monkey's invulnerability by plunging his feet into boiling oil. In Chinese legends Monkey corresponds to a Puck or Robin Goodfellow in England. He is a naughty character who successfully goes against the establishment whether human or divine.

His exploits were told in a long saga called the "Journey to the West" which described the adventures of the monk, Yuen Tsong, who went to India to fetch the Buddhist scriptures. This was a true story but fostered a huge collection of legendary tales and characters of whom the Monkey is one. He stole the Peaches of Immortality from Heaven and thereby made himself indestructible. In other gory feats at the festival to celebrate his birthday, mediums climb ladders with rungs made of sharp knives, cut their tongues with a sword and bite into porcelain cups and plates, stick sharp razors through their cheeks and run on burning charcoals.

The Kowloon Peninsula

1995

Shot from Fei Ngo Shan (Kowloon Peak). A favourite
view for photographs, not least because it is possible to drive
a good way up the mountain with all the camera equipment.
From here the view encompasses Tsz Wan Shan on the right,
the vast housing estates of Choi Hung and Ngau Tau Kok, and
part of Kowloon Bay on the left. The yellow line across the
photograph shows an aircraft has just landed at Kai Tak airport

明月到窗籠冊　開窗臨海面

NEW TERRITORIES

Clearwater Bay Golf and Country Club

1996

Clearwater Bay golf course and Clearwater Bay Peninsula, with 344-metre high Junk Peak (Tiu Yue Yung) rising gracefully from the bay. The awe-inspiring 14th hole is set against a backdrop of the South China Sea. If you slice the ball only slightly here, it will meet a watery grave. This wonderfully positioned club is the largest in the territory, covering a site of 145 hectares and boasting an 18-hole course and a second nine-hole golf course, as well as marina club, pool and luxury clubhouse. Established in 1982 amid gloomy predictions for its future, the pessimists have been proved hopelessly wrong; corporate debentures, which could be bought for just HK$75,000 in 1984, are now selling for well over HK$2 million.

PREVIOUS PAGE
North Sai Kung

1995

Three Fathoms Cove (Kei Ling Ha Hoi) with the tiny island of Wu Chau in the centre.

Clearwater Bay Beach

1996

Sunday at Clearwater Bay Beach (Tsing Shui Wan)
on the Sai Kung Peninsula. This area in the eastern
New Territories is one of the most unspoilt and
breathtakingly beautiful in the territory.

Tin Hau Festival

1985

Part of a flotilla of gaily decorated lighters and junks make
their way towards the temple at Joss House Bay on the
23rd day of the 3rd moon.

OVERLEAF
Hung Shing Kung's birthday

1976

An elaborate shrine, or *fa-pau*, constructed of bamboo and
paper, is brought by boat to the festival celebrating Hung
Shing Kung's birthday at Kau Sai Island. A favourite god
amongst Hong Kong's seafarers, Hung Shing Kung is
believed by some followers to be the Dragon King of the
Southern Seas, while others claim he was a Tang Dynasty
official, much admired for his accurate weather forecasts.
But these vague credentials in no way detract from the jovial
annual birthday celebrations held in Hung Shing Kung
temples in several fishing communities throughout
the territory.

Tin Hau Festival

1993

A dancing lion leads the way as a towering floral *fa-pau* is presented for
blessing in front of a matshed temple in Castle Peak, Tuen Mun.

Fish Farms

1996

Fish farms at Tai Wong Kung, Clearwater Bay. Marine fish farming is a
well-established industry around the coast of the eastern New Territories.

RIGHT

Hebe Haven

1984

Diced root vegetables are dried in the sun before being pickled at a farm
in Hebe Haven, Sai Kung.

Mainland junks

1981

This wonderful flotilla of junks from Amoy assembled in Joss House Bay, after sailing south
to escape the threat of an earthquake. Hong Kong police cordoned off the boats for the
several days they remained in the territory, and, since the earthquake on the mainland never
materialized, an aura of mystery has remained around the whole episode.

Live red snapper

1996

Live red snapper, a popular local delicacy for sale in
a wholesale fish market in Castle Peak.

RIGHT
Sai Kung Peninsula

1995

Empty rocky promontories and inlets sheltering
small fishing communities still characterize the
beautiful High Island Reservoir area. This view from
the Sai Kung Man Yee Road, which borders the
reservoir, looks southwest across Rocky Harbour
(Leung Shuen Wan Hoi), with the fishing village of
Sha Kiu Tau in the middle distance, and the
rugged silhouette of Bluff Island (Sha Tong
Hau Shan) behind.

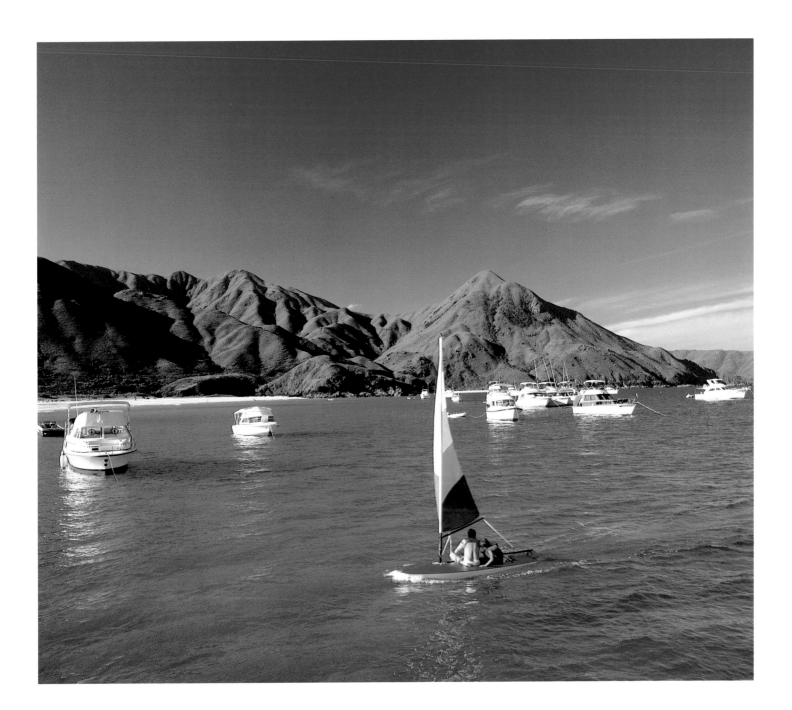

Tai Long Wan

1986

This magnificent aerial view of Tai Long Wan (literally, Big Wave Bay) is one of the very few Hong Kong vistas which has hardly changed in 26 years. On Sundays the bay becomes full of pleasure craft and people enjoying the clean water and even occasional surf. Memories of wonderful tranquil days spent here linger on forever.

Tat Hong Channel

1977

Four junks from the mainland head for China under full sail through this channel which is east of Hong Kong Island. Cape Collinson is in the background.

RIGHT
Inner Port Shelter, Sai Kung

1996

This view of one of Hong Kong's most beautiful areas is from the main dam of High Island, looking towards Sai Kung with Urn Island (Tai Tau Chau) and Kau Sai Chau, now the site of Hong Kong's first public golf couse, on the left. Those lucky enough to hire or own boats weekend overnight in the calm bays along the shore. It was a favourite water skiing place.

OVERLEAF
Sai Kung Peninsula

1995

From Sai Kung Man Yee Road, looking south across the inlet of Pak Lap Tsai to the South China Sea. The road is part of the MacLehose Trail, the 100-km cross-country trail, named after one of Hong Kong's most admired Governors (1971-1982), which leads walkers through some of Hong Kong's most spectacular mountainous terrain.

Tin Hau Temple, Tap Mun Island

1996

Intricate figures of gods, folklore characters and lucky symbols, made in the famous
Shek Wan potteries of South China, are traditional features of Chinese temple roofs.
This particularly impressive line-up tops off the Tin Hau Temple on Tap Mun Chau, the small,
peaceful island that lies at the convergence of Tolo and Long Harbours in the northeast of
the territory. The temple is one of the most beautiful and best preserved of Hong Kong's
many temples dedicated to the sea goddess and Queen of Heaven, Tin Hau. The richly
ornamented statue of her (right) is the focal point inside.

Yim Tin Tsai fish farm

1994

The view looks south across Tolo Harbour with the Chinese University on the hillside in the distance. Many of the more accessible villages in this area have become dormitory towns, but here people still earn a living from farming and fishing, On the right, fish on sale in markets in the New Territories. Cantonese fish dishes depend on the freshest of ingredients and ideally the fish must be live when bought. With expert timing, and masterful understanding of natural flavours, they are typically steamed in a sauce of oil, fresh ginger and green onions, or lightly stir-fried, to create possibly the world's greatest seafood cuisine.

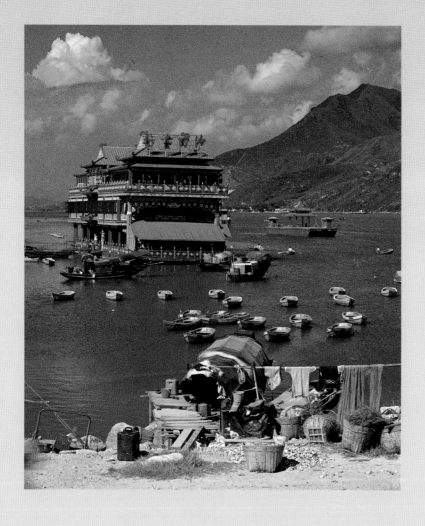

Sha Tin
1971 & 1995

In 1971, Sha Tin was a fishing town, its harbour dotted with small leisure boats, and providing anchorage for a floating restaurant. Now, as a result of a major government-led scheme to build a network of new towns in the New Territories, the harbour has been filled in and half a million people live in this massive satellite town. By 1998, 700,000 people will live there - over half of them in public housing. The new Sha Tin, photographed from the air in 1995, has many of the trappings of an independent town, with shopping centres, schools, a famous racecourse with Penfold Park in the centre, museum, concert hall and university. The old floating restaurant has been 'anchored' to the reclaimed land.

Ladies' Day at Sha Tin Racecourse
1996

71,200 people turned up on November 16
to watch nine races in each of which lady
jockeys were competing. They spent
HK$1.326 billion (£106,000,000) betting on
these nine races. This phenomenal sum
easily exceeds the turnover of any other
racecourse in the world. The feature race
was the Ladies' Purse, first run in 1863.
Traditionally, gold sovereigns were
presented to the winning parties by an
unmarried daughter of one of Hong Kong's
dignitaries but since 1990, lunar year gold
coins have replaced them. The racecourse
was opened in 1978. It is equipped with
every conceivable modern luxury including
piped music in the stables and heated
swimming pools for the horses. It has the
world's biggest trackside video matrix which
provides slow motion film and instant
replays of the races, as well as all the
information of the betting and odds in two
languages. The 250 acres of reclaimed land
accommodates three tracks, stands for
83,000 racegoers and a central public park.

Sai Kung
1989

An old lady tending cows near the village of Ko Tung Ha Yeung in Sai Kung.

BOTTOM LEFT
Ta Kwu Ling
1996

A farmhand from mainland China at work in the closed area of Ta Kwu Ling along the Chinese border.

FAR LEFT
Tai Po Kau
1971

Gathering seaweed by the roadside at Tai Po Kau. The shallow waters in this picture have gone, engulfed by a massive reclamation project which provided land for the new town of Tai Po, now home to 258,000 people.

Sha Lo Tung Valley

1989 & 1993

A left-over from another era, the traditional Hakka village of Cheung Uk lies in the unspoilt Sha Lo Tung Valley, a few miles northeast of the Tai Po Road. Twenty years ago Cheung Uk had 450 inhabitants; now the population has dwindled to a few old ladies who tend the ancestral hall. The valley itself, enclosed on all sides so that it is invisible below, is home to a rich variety of flora and fauna, and its meandering stream is the only unpolluted, slow-flowing stream in the entire territory. But the valley's future is uncertain; a long drawn-out battle between conservationists and former residents who would like to develop the site into a luxury residential estate and golf course is still to be resolved.

Old lady of Tsuen Wan

1980

Hong Kong's old people have not always been well catered for in fast changing Hong Kong, but this old lady was living in a special home where she could retain some of her self-sufficiency through the support of the Buddhist nuns of Chuk Lam Monastery, near Tsuen Wan.

FAR LEFT

Temple at Nam Chung

1989

This is one of my favourite photographs as it was a lovely surprise to find this little temple in an isolated place and in such wonderful light. The temple is located near Starling Inlet (Sha Tau Kok Hoi). I have since returned and it has been cleaned up and painted which has sadly destroyed all the atmosphere seen in the old photograph.

Luk Keng duck farm

1992

A duck farm in an idyllic setting near Starling Inlet (Sha Tau Kok Hoi). Like other traditional forms of farming in Hong Kong, duck production is declining, and much of the excellent duck consumed in Hong Kong's restaurants is now imported.

FAR RIGHT
Sheung Shui
1977

A small boy catches up on his homework while waiting for his school bus near the village. The Chinese characters translate as "The Bridge for the Convenience of my Mother". It was built in 1710 by Tang Chuen Yuen to enable his mother to visit her grandchildren across the stream.

FAR BOTTOM RIGHT
Man Shek Tong, Sheung Shui
1977

This is the main ancestral hall of the Lui Clan. It is a three hall type building and believed to date from 1751. It has the richest wood carvings of ancestral halls in the territory and has recently been totally renovated. At this time it housed a temporary primary school, which has long since moved to new premises. Twenty-five years ago there were barely enough school places in Hong Kong to allow every child a primary education. Educational opportunities have improved dramatically at all levels, and now a quarter of school leavers go on to tertiary education in the territory.

Chinese New Year Harvest

1996

The delicate peach blossoms are the most sought-after decorative and auspicious plants at Chinese New Year; peachwood is viewed as a potent enemy of demons and the peach itself is an emblem of longevity. It is vital the flowers open just at the right moment and girls from across the border are employed in the weeks before the New Year festival to pick off any blossoms that might flower too early. The orange trees are also auspicious at New Year as the Chinese name for them is "Gat" which means "Good Fortune". They produce bitter kumquats, but the dried skin is used as a condiment in many dishes or as confectionery.

Lau Fau Shan, Deep Bay
1975

A farmer has commandeered the services of all his family, down to the very youngest,
to help prepare the radish (*law bak*) crop for the markets of Kowloon.

RIGHT
Green Organic Farm
1995

The 'Produce Green Organic Farm' near Loi Tung was established by a foundation to help
preserve traditional, chemical-free, methods of farming. Part of the land is farmed by
enthusiasts, and the rest is leased to full-time farmers who raise produce to sell to the 35,000
visitors who pass through each year. The rice paddy here is almost the last in the territory.

Ha Tsuen Ta Chiu Festival

1976

Elders waiting to greet VIP visitors at the festival. This large-scale Taoist festival, held just once every ten years in the village of Ha Tsuen near Yuen Long, ambitiously aims to wipe out evil in the whole area, restore peace, and renew life for the entire population. The event is so important that emigrants return to Hong Kong especially to participate in this festival which can last up to a week. The Taoist priests are reading the names of all member villagers from the long scroll. These festivals are held all over the New Territories. At Lam Tsuen in 1981, 23 villages took part, the matshed theatre held 3,000 people, more than a thousand came back from Europe and the name list totalled nearly 7,000.

OUTLYING ISLANDS

Lamma Island
1980

A lone junk makes its way past Lamma Island, with the islands of the South China Sea in the distance. The preceding page shows the island from a helicopter hovering near Yung Shue Bay; the craggy ribbon of island stretching away to the northeast. In the distance on Hong Kong Island, across the busy shipping lanes of the Lamma Channel, can be seen the highrises of Western, Pokfulam and Aberdeen. Lamma is the third largest island in the territory, after Lantau and Hong Kong, but has largely escaped development; no roads link the small pockets of habitation where some 8,000 people live.

RIGHT
Fat Tong Mun
1975

On a rare becalmed sea, a junk is oared through Fat Tong Mun, the narrow channel of water between the island of Tung Lung Chau and the Clearwater Bay Peninsula. One of the most attractive features of these wonderful butterflies of the sea were the sails - invariably patched in different colours or full of holes - yet still able to propel the craft long distances.

Hei Ling Chau

1973

Fishing over, the nets gathered and sails furled, the children are left to do acrobatics in the rigging. In the background is Hei Ling Chau, a small island off Lantau.

LEFT
Silvermine Bay, Lantau

1996

Two ferries leave Silvermine Bay (Ngan Kwong Wan) on Lantau Island. In the distance is Hong Kong Island, with Victoria Peak and the buildings of Western and Pokfulam clearly visible. On the left in the middle distance, is the smaller island of Peng Chau, a port of call for ferries en route from Lantau to Central.

Lantau Island

1973

Farmers could still be seen tilling the soil with a wooden plough drawn by
a buffalo in the 1970s. This farm and village, now totally abandoned, was at
Ha Keng on the Chi Ma Wan Peninsula.

Lantau Link, Kap Shui Mun Bridge

1998

Part of the 34 km direct road and rail network leading to Hong Kong
International Airport at Chek Lap Kok. Ma Wan Island is in the centre and
Ting Kau Bridge, which marks the beginning of the new Route 3 Toll Road
through Tai Lam Tunnel on to Yuen Long, is on the far left.

Chek Lap Kok Terminal

1998

Only 9 years from start to finish, but costing US$20 Billion, Hong Kong's new airport was
the largest infrastructure project ever undertaken globally. Designed by Sir Norman Foster,
the terminal building is the biggest covered structure in the world.

LEFT

Silvermine Bay, Lantau

1995

A short walk from the ferry is this relic of the past, probably part of an old fortified village.

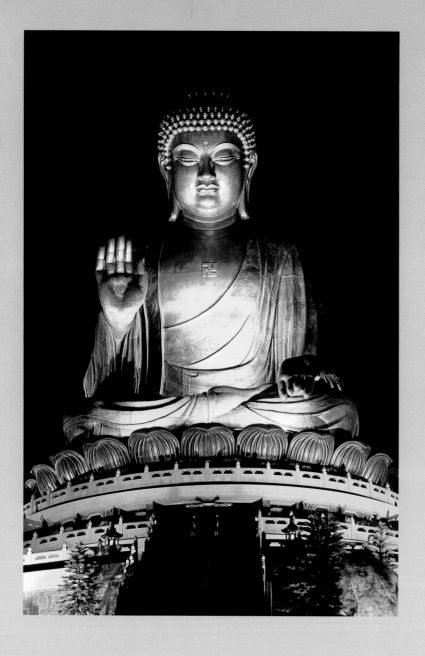

Po Lin Monastery, Lantau

1995

The world's largest seated, outdoor, bronze Buddha dominates
the dramatic mountainous landscape above the monastery.
Completed in 1993, it took six years, and HK$70 million, to create
this 26.4 metre-high bronze. The statue weighs 202 tonnes, and sits
on a lotus throne on top of a three-platformed altar, with 268 steps
leading up to it. The monks at Po Lin designed the Buddha, but
they had help in construction from mainland Chinese engineers.
The lights which illuminate the Buddha so spectacularly are only
turned on once or twice a month on auspicious days because the
electricity costs are so high. The small temple of Wei To on the right
acts as an entrance gate to the monastery.

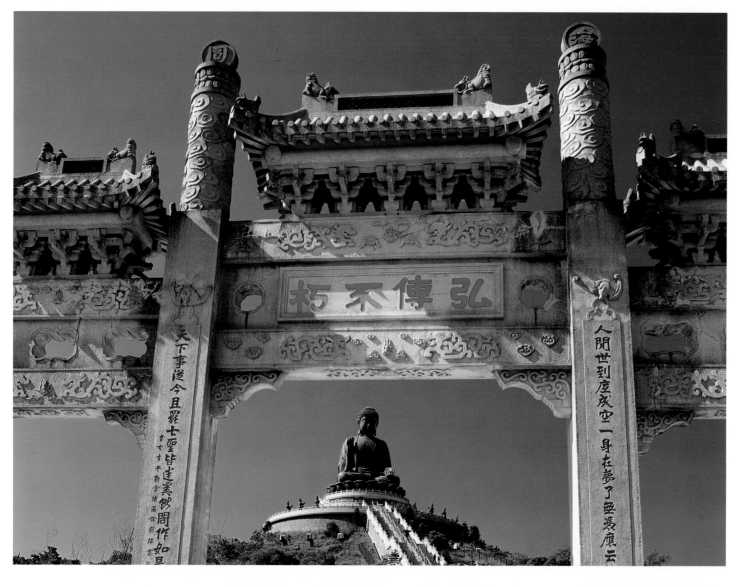

Po Lin Monastery

1996

The Giant Buddha, and interiors at the
Po Lin Monastery, Lantau Island. Po Lin means
"Precious Lotus", the lotus flower being the symbol
of the Buddhist faith. The affluent monastery
complex is relatively new; most of it has been built
since 1970, although the first three monks took up
residence in a few stone huts on this site in 1905.

Today the monastery is a large and thriving
community with thousands of visitors arriving each
day to see the Buddha. Inside the ornate two-storey
main temple, which is dedicated to the Three
Precious Buddhas, are clusters of tasselled lanterns
hung from the richly carved and painted arched
roof, gilded shrines, and long hangings of red and
yellow embroidery. The large brass bell, cast in
1965, is engraved with the names of the donors
in red characters.

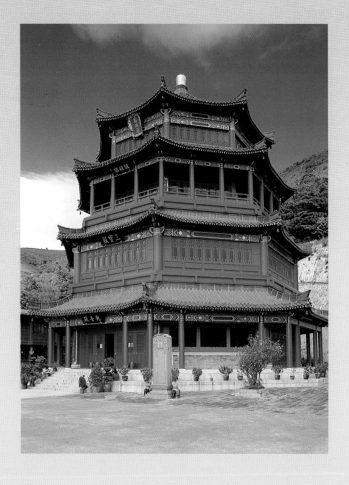

Kwun Yum Temple, Lantau

1995

Kwun Yum, the Buddhist Goddess of Mercy, is loved
by both Taoists and Buddhists, and many temples
are dedicated to her in Hong Kong. But this one,
painstakingly restored in 1995 with no expense
spared by a wealthy Hong Kong businessman, is
one of the most beautiful. Craftsmen were brought
from China to ensure that every detail of the building
was of the highest quality. The original site was
granted by Sir Cecil Clementi (Governor of Hong
Kong 1925-1930) to his favourite amah, who built
a small temple here.

Tai O, Lantau

1995

An anachronistic rope-drawn ferry used to connect the two sides of the village divided by a creek. The sampan which ferried passengers across the narrow creek cost 50 cents a crossing and survived until late 1996 when it was superseded by a cement bridge.

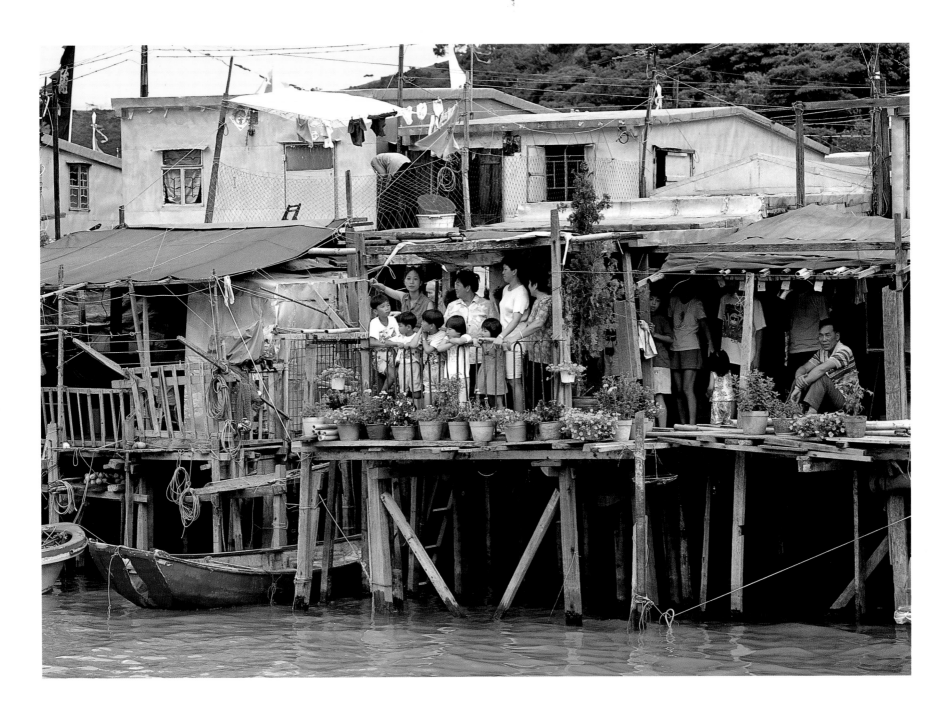

Tai O, Lantau

1995

The village, on the western tip of Lantau, is a strongly traditional fishing
community, where ramshackle houses on stilts spill out over the creek.
The family are watching the dragon boat racing. The row of pot plants adds
a charming homely touch to the balcony of this precarious-looking dwelling.

Dragon Boat Races in Tai O, Lantau

1995

Hundreds of fire crackers explode to mark the start of the races, with a noise so deafening, it must leave those standing nearby unable to hear properly for weeks to come. Fire crackers have been banned in Hong Kong since the 1967 riots when gun powder normally used for these small explosions was diverted for use in bombs. Nonetheless, they can still be seen - or heard - on festive occasions in remote corners of the territory. Tai O has always been a fishing village but before 1841 it was notorious as a pirate haven.

Tai O, Lantau

1995

This is one of the most beautiful places in Hong Kong to view dragon boat
racing as the village is very traditional, there are almost no foreign visitors
and the setting is unique.

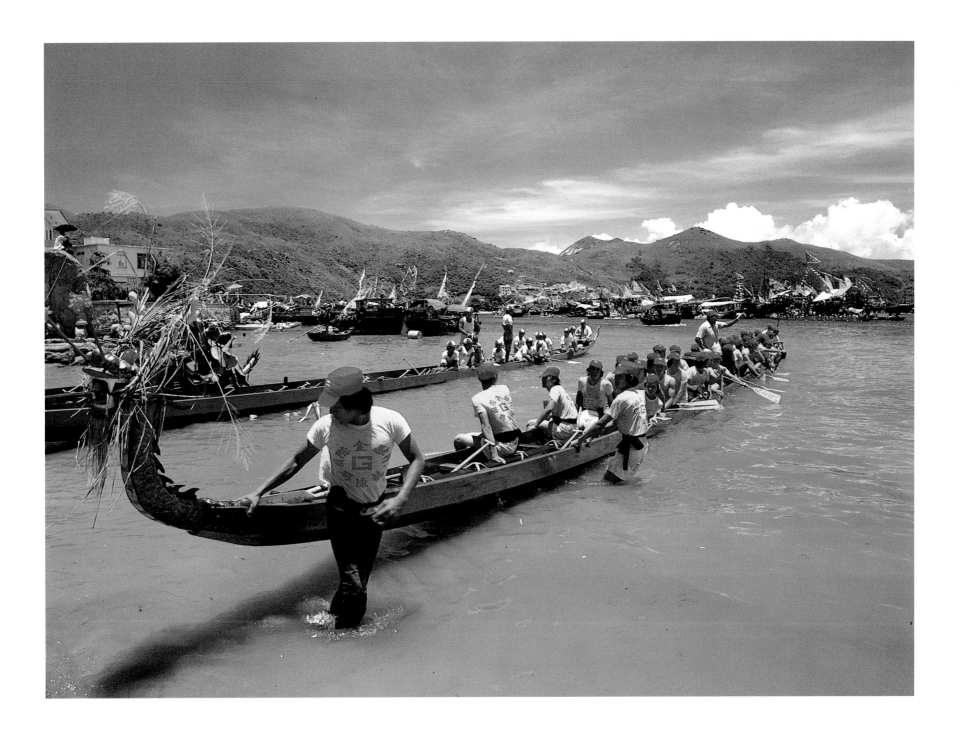

Dragon boats blessing

1988

Before racing gets underway, dragon boats come to shore for blessing at
the temple in Luk Chau Bay on the east side of Lamma Island.

Tai O
1995

Wearing the flat-crowned Tanka hat favoured by many of Hong Kong's fishing community, a woman sorts through a basket of dried shrimps. Tai O reputedly has the finest quality salt-dried fish in Hong Kong.

RIGHT
Salt-dried fish
1995

A typical array of salt-dried fish found in shops through-out the territory.

Tai O

1994

The sun sets behind fishing boats at anchor in Tai O, the heart of Lantau's fishing industry.

RIGHT
Pui O

1978

Hong Kong's glorious patchwork landscape of rice paddies has virtually disappeared.
Vegetable growing is much more profitable and the amount of land devoted to rice had
dropped from over 9,000 hectares in 1954 to less than 10 hectares by the end of the 1980s.

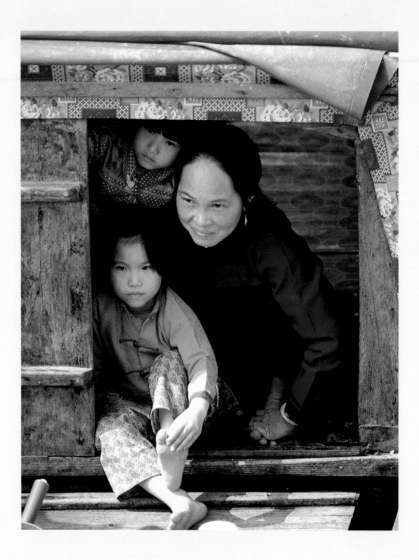

Tanka family, Tap Mun

1986

The Tanka were said to be exiled to the sea for plotting against a Sung Dynasty emperor who decreed that their descendants should never again live on land. Families lived, gave birth and died in their tiny sampans and old junks.

LEFT

Hei Ling Chau

1973

This remains one of my all-time favourite photographs. It was taken on a balmy May evening during a boat picnic to Lantau. The sun is setting over Sunset Peak and the fishing family are on their last catch of the day,

Cheung Chau

1984

Fishing boats at anchor on this small, densely populated island, with an area of just
2.3 square kilometres, to the southwest of Hong Kong Island. Traditionally its people have
focused on fishing, with a little piracy and smuggling on the side, but increasingly
commuters who work in Hong Kong have set up home here.

LEFT
Cheung Chau Bun Festival

1976

The small Taoist shrine, erected especially for the festival, is constructed out of hanging
fabrics and paintings depicting deities and revered historical characters. Its guardian is
taking a smoking break - probably one of the last generation in Hong Kong to use
traditional bamboo pipes.

Cheung Chau Bun Festival

1980s

The six-day festival is celebrated in May with a unique procession. Three vast wooden towers, each covered with some 5,000 white buns stamped with a goodwill message, are erected near the Pak Tai Temple. Their purpose is to appease the hungry spirits of pirate victims, whose mutilated bodies were found in the 1880s on the island. The festival also gives thanks to Pak Tai, Emperor of the North and God of the Sea, for protecting the islanders since the 1770s from various plagues. The festivities include Chinese opera, lion dances, stilt dances and a fabulous procession, featuring many legendary figures as well as more contemporary celebrities.

OVERLEAF

The Float Procession

1980s

The young children held aloft in Cheung Chau's famous street processions are always the stars of the island's Bun Festival. Aged between five and eight, they are supported on frames and carried shoulder-high throughout the whole parade to create an elaborate, often whimsical, tableau representing characters in history or mythology. Decked out in thick makeup, with heavy costumes and headgear, the children have to spend some four hours, motionless, in the baking sun - small wonder their faces are not always ecstatic.

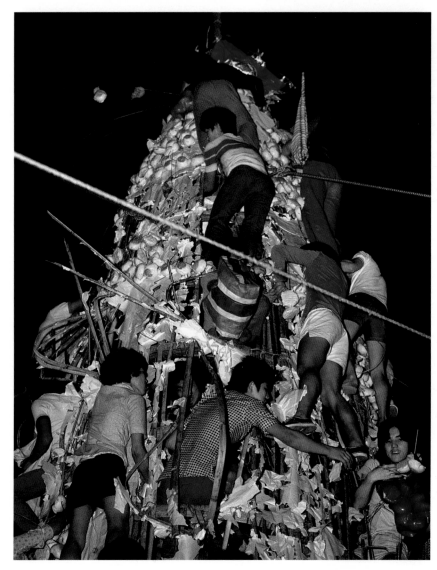

Cheung Chau Bun Festival

1974

The traditional climax of the six-day festival used to be a midnight scramble up 20-metre towers of buns. The three huge conical bamboo and paper towers, covered from top to bottom in layers of pink and white buns, are pictured. The buns - part of a grand offering to the ghosts which the festival is attempting to appease - are a symbol of good fortune and a talisman against sickness for whoever manages to grab one. The higher the bun, the greater the luck it was supposed to bring. In the mad dash up the towers by the young men at the festival, it took just a few minutes to strip them bare of buns. The practice was banned officially after one of the towers collapsed in the assault, even though no-one was hurt. Nowadays the buns are distributed to orderly queues the next morning.

INDEX

LEFT
Sunset over Lantau Island
1996

Sunset over the Western Harbour where cargo ships are anchored, waiting
to load or offload their goods. To the right is the new suspension bridge
linking Hong Kong and Kowloon to Chek Lap Kok airport.

TECHNICAL BACKGROUND

Almost all of the photographs taken after 1991 are on Fujichrome Velvia. Prior to this I used Kodachrome for most of the 35mm photographs and Ektachrome or Agfachrome for the larger formats. The reason for the switch to Velvia was principally because it was the first film to match and surpass the vivid colours and saturation of Kodachrome, but also because it could be processed and back in one's hands within two hours. Kodachrome had to be sent to Australia and two weeks would pass before the results came back.

The problem with Velvia, as with Kodachrome, is the slow speed. As I used to do a lot of aerial photography from vibrating helicopters with polarising filters which cut the speed by a further 60%, this meant I needed a very firm and steady hand. Many photographs would be ruined by minute camera shake. However, there have been no other films which can match the brilliant, intense colours combined with superb sharpness of these two films.

The photographs of the fishermen on page xxvi and page 184 would not have been possible on colour transparency films such as Kodachrome or Velvia. These were shot on colour negative film, which has a much greater latitude, and I was therefore able to expose for the shadows and faces of the fishermen and prevent the background from washing out which would have happened on transparency or diapositive film.

Hong Kong is a photographer's heaven in that it is full of light and colour, but it is not always an easy place to photograph. The weather is often unconducive to photography as there are very few times of the year when the air is clear. Even back in the 1970s you had to pick your days very carefully. On many occasions, laden down with camera equipment, I have trekked across to the Peak on a clear fine day, only to find that within minutes grey black clouds appeared from nowhere. Now that I am living in London and visit Hong Kong sporadically these problems become even more acute.

The photography of people has never been easy in Hong Kong. In earlier days one was constantly abused and almost attacked if one pointed a camera at people, particularly simple folk living in country areas and on the outlying islands. The old suspicion that a photograph or camera robbed the subject of its soul was still strongly entrenched when I started photographing Hong Kong. Despite these minor problems Hong Kong has been a very rewarding and exciting place to record, with its continual changes and developments and its wonderful situation next to the sea.

Captions for pages 124 & 125
Aerial Patterns

1. 1988. Aberdeen: fishing boats at anchor.
2. 1975. Paddy field and old village, Yuen Long.
3. 1986. Fish Farm, near Tap Mun Island, Long Harbour.
4. 1994. Previously "Air House", it was the first private residence to be sold for $1 million and is now worth hundreds of millions.
5. 1980. A junk, the butterfly of the China Seas.
6. 1986. The Mai Po Marshes, near Yuen Long, famous for their bird population.
7. 1995. Shenzhen in China, across the river. The duck and fish farms are in Hong Kong.
8. 1996. A pool in Repulse Bay.
9. 1994. The New Territories is rapidly becoming a container park. This is near Tuen Mun.
10. 1993. Rollercoaster at Ocean Park which first opened in 1977 and has had more than 37 million visitors since then.
11. 1985. The New Territories. Farms near Fanling.
12. 1993. The Middle Kingdom, Ocean Park, a Chinese cultural village that recreates 5,000 years of Chinese history.
13. 1994. Repulse Bay Beach on a Saturday.
14. 1994. A Star Ferry. The Star Ferry Company was founded in 1897 by a Parsee, Dorabjee Nowrojee, who arrived a cook and ended up the prosperous owner of King Edward Hotel, reputedly the best in town. 96,000 people still cross the harbour by Star Ferry every day. There are 12 ferries in operation.
15. 1994. The Typhoon Shelter at Sham Wan, Aberdeen.
16. 1988. Port Shelter and Rocky Harbour, Sai Kung.
17. 1979. The boat building yards at Shum Wan, Aberdeen.
18. 1993. Fairview Gardens, Yuen Long, New Territories.

Hong Kong SAR

N ↑

Scale 1: 200 000

0   2   4   6   8   10 kms

0   2   4   6 miles

CHINA

Deep Bay

Mai Po Marshes

Lau Fau Shan

Nam Sang
Wai

Tin Shui
Wai

Yuen
Long

Kam Tin

NE
TERRITO

Tuen
Mun

*Tai Lam
Chung
Reservoir*

▲ 507

*Castle
Peak
583*

Ma Wan

Urmston Road

*Tsing Ma
Bridge*

Kap Shui
Mun Bridge

The Brothers

Legend

	Country Park
———	Main Road
———	Secondary Road
·········	Tunnel
▬▬▬	Railway
- - - -	Light Railway
———	Airport Rail Link
- - - -	Ferry
	Urban Area
	Planned reclamation
▲	Peak (height in meters)
✈	Hong Kong Int'l Airport

✈
Hong Kong
International Airport

Discovery
Bay

Peng Chau

Ka
C

Tung
Chung

Mui Wo

Silvermine Bay

Sunshine
Island

Lantau

Island

Po Lin ●
Monastery

*Lantau
Peak*
▲
933

▲ *Sunset
Peak*
869

Tai O

Hei Ling
Chau

West Lamma Channel

Fan Lau

Cheung
Chau

Lantau Channel

Shek Kwu
Chau

Soko Islands